HOLINESS:
MAN'S SUPREME DESTINY

THE LADDER OF DIVINE ASCENT
Man's Heavenward Ascent as
portrayed in Orthodox iconography.

HOLINESS:
MAN'S SUPREME DESTINY

Four Orthodox Homilies in which are
Discussed the Concept of Holiness, Hunger
for Holiness, and Striving for Holiness

By

CONSTANTINE CAVARNOS

INSTITUTE FOR BYZANTINE
AND MODERN GREEK STUDIES
115 Gilbert Road
Belmont, Massachusetts 02478-2200
U.S.A.

On the front cover: *Icon of The Transfiguration of Christ*, by Photios Kontoglou. Holy Transfiguration Monastery, Brookline, Massachusetts. Used with permission.

First Edition, 2001
All Rights Reserved
Copyright, © 2001 by Constantine Cavarnos
Published by THE INSTITUTE FOR BYZANTINE
AND MODERN GREEK STUDIES, INC.
115 Gilbert Road
Belmont, Massachusetts 02478-2200

Library of Congress Control Number: 2001 132810

Printed in the United States of America

Clothbound ISBN 1-884729-64-9
Paperbound ISBN 1-884729-65-7

CONTENTS

LIST OF ILLUSTRATIONS

PREFACE

This book is comprised of four homilies that were written for Orthodox audiences in different parts of the United States. The idea of publishing them together was not in my mind at the time I wrote them. Recently, I decided to publish them in book form and, thus, make them available to the general reading public who are interested in Orthodox Christian spirituality. To this end, I arranged them so that they follow each other in the appropriate sequence. All four of the homilies were delivered during the last decade of the twentieth century.

"Hunger for Holiness", Chapter One, was delivered in the great hall of Holy Apostles Greek Orthodox Church in Westchester, Illinois. It was the keynote speech at "A Celebration of Orthodox Books" which took place from March 3 to March 10, 1991, and was sponsored by "The Christian Education Commission Under the Guidance of the Diocese of Chicago." This homily was published in 1995 as a monograph by the Center for Traditionalist Orthodox Studies in Etna, California. In presenting it in this book, I have left out certain paragraphs and incorporated them in the second chapter, as more appropriate there.

"Striving for Holiness", Chapter Two, was sponsored by the Orthodox Church of America, Diocese of the South, at its Twenty-first Diocesan Assembly held in Miami, Florida, July 7-9, 1998. It was the keynote address which was delivered on July 9 at the hall of the Orthodox Cathedral of Christ the Savior.

"St. Nectarios' Counsels for Spiritual Strivers", Chapter Three, is a lecture which I delvered on March 30, 1994 at Holy Cross Greek Orthodox School of Theology in Brookline, Massachusetts, at a seminar course on St. Nectarios of Aegina directed by the Very Reverend Father Cleopas Strongyllis and was attended by the seniors of the School.

The last chapter, "Spiritual Strivers' Church in the Home," is an address to a Greek-speaking audience at the Church of Saint George in Lynn, Massachusetts, given at the invitation of the priest of the parish, Father George Tsoucalas. It was delivered on the Fifth Sunday of Great Lent, March 13, 1997. This particular homily was originally written in Greek and published as a series of articles in the monthly periodical *Ho Poimen* (*The Shepherd*) of the Holy Metropolis of Mytilene, Greece. The following year, it was translated into English by Dr. Constantine Kokenes of Atlanta, Georgia, and was published as Monograph No. 1 by the journal *Divine Ascent* at Point Reyes Station, California. In order to include that translation in this book, I have gone over the whole translation and made many revisions for a more precise rendering of the Greek text. The latter appeared in the form of an 18-page booklet that was published in 1999 by the Institute for Byzantine and Modern Greek Studies.

I owe many thanks to the following dedicated Orthodox priests who cordially invited me to speak and thus occasioned the writing and delivery of these homilies: Reverend Fathers William Chiganos of Westchester, Illinois, Philip Reese of Miami, Florida, Cleopas Strongyllis of Brookline, Massachusetts (now at Corona, New York), and George Tsoucalas of Lynn, Massachusetts. I am also very grateful to Reverend Father Joseph Frawley of West Point, New York, for having carefully gone over the whole manuscript and suggested many improvements in expression.

Holiness: Man's Supreme Destiny constitutes a sequel to my book *Paths and Means to Holiness,* which has been translated into Finnish and Greek and published in Finland and Greece. These books complement one another, dealing with different aspects of the same very important subject of holiness. Both are addressed to persons who are interested in developing spiritually and aspire to make the highest spiritual attainments: purity, likeness, to God, and union with Him, the Fount of holiness.

CONSTANTINE CAVARNOS

Belmont, Massachusetts
July, 2001

CHRIST THE PANTOCRATOR
Panel icon in the Church of St. Therapon, Mytilene.
Fourteenth Century.

CHAPTER ONE

Hunger for Holiness*

There are many references to hunger in the New Testament. Some of them are to *physical* hunger, while others are to *spiritual* hunger. In the Gospel according to Matthew, Chapter 4, verse 2, we read that Christ "fasted forty days and forty nights and afterward He was *hungry* [*epeínase*]." The second reference, which appears in the Sermon on the Mount, in Chapter 5, is to spiritual hunger. Christ says: "Blessed are those who *hunger* and thirst for righteousness, for they shall be satisfied" (5:6).

The *nature* of these two kinds of hunger, the physical and the spiritual, is not explained in the New Testament. For everyone has a vivid experiential knowledge of physical hunger,

* Speech on March 3, 1991, at "A Celebration of Orthodox Books" in the great hall of Holy Apostles Greek Orthodox Church in Westchester, Illinois, in the presence of the Most Reverend Metropolitan Iakovos of Chicago.

and has at least an inkling of what is meant by hunger for righteousness. For the purpose of this discourse, however, it will be very helpful to attempt an *analysis* of their nature.

Introspection discloses, as the philosopher Plato points out in his *Republic*, that physical hunger (*peína*) is a state of *emptiness* (*kénosis*) of the bodily condition.[1] The same is true, he notes, of thirst (*dípsa*). The *emptiness* experienced in hunger and thirst, Plato observes in another dialogue, the *Philebus*, is accompanied by *pain* (*lype*). This pain gives rise to the *desire* (*epithymía*) of the *opposite* of what one feels.[2] A hungry person feels *emptiness and pain* and *desires* being *filled* (*pleróseos*) with food, while a thirsty person feels another kind of emptiness and pain, and desires to be filled with drink. Thus, hunger and thirst are resolvable into three things: (1) a feeling of emptiness;(2) a feeling of pain; and (3) a desire for food and drink, respectively. The satisfaction of hunger and thirst results in a feeling of *fullness* and *pleasure* (*hedoné*) and the cessation of desire.

I have spoken of thirst as well as of hunger, because Plato often discussed them together, and because our Lord Jesus, too, mentions them together in His Sermon on the Mount as well as elsewhere. But whereas Plato speaks only of *physical* hunger and thirst, Christ speaks of *both physical and spiritual* hunger and thirst.

Spiritual hunger and thirst are purely states of the psyche, the soul. They have nothing to do with the body. They arise

---

[1] *Republic*, IV. 437D, IX. 585.
[2] *Philebus*, 31E-34E.

in the soul and are directed towards something incorporeal. In the Sermon on the Mount, their object is said to be righteousness (*dikaiosyne*): something non-physical, spiritual. St. Gregory of Nyssa, in his treatise *Concerning Perfection*, identifies righteousness and inner peace with the whole of virtue ("*Diá tes dikaiosynes te kai eirénes pásas oímai dein tas aretás ennoeín*").[1]

Very significant in Christ's statement is His promise that those who hunger and thirst for righteousness *will find fulfillment* of their hunger and thirst for it: "They shall be filled." This statement preserves the analogy between spiritual and physical hunger and thirst.

The parallelism between physical and spiritual hunger and thirst is vividly exemplified in St. Nectarios' discussion of the desire for the Supreme Good, that is, for God. In his book *Sketch Concerning Man*, this great twentieth-century Saint speaks of the emptiness (*to kenón*) in the heart of man, of the pain (*álgos*) in it, and of the heart's strong desire (*epithymía*) or thirst to enjoy the Supreme Good. There is, he says, an emptiness in the heart of man, in his emotional center. This emptiness, he explains, can be satisfied neither by material wealth, nor by worldly glory, nor by anything else on earth that is regarded as good. It cannot be satisfied by worldly goods, because the soul, being spiritual in nature and immortal, has infinite spiritual longings. Therefore, "she longs for

---

[1] *Perí Teleiótetos (De Perfectione), in Gregorii Nysseni Opera*, Vol. VIII, Pars I, ed. Wernerus Jaeger, Leiden, 1952, p. 208.

and seeks, like a thirsty deer, the enjoyment of the Highest Good," God.[1]

St. Nectarios' statements bring to mind a famous remark which St. Augustine makes at the beginning of his *Confessions*. Addressing himself to God, Augustine says: "Thou madest us for Thyself, and our heart is restless until it repose in Thee."

That God alone can fill the great emptiness in us, satisfy our spiritual hunger, is taught by the God-Man Christ Himself. In the Gospel according to John, Christ says: "I am the bread of life: he that cometh to Me shall never hunger; and he that believeth in Me shall never thirst" (6:35; cf. 4:14 and Revelation, 7:15-16).

Our seeking to fill the great emptiness within us by the awakening in our soul of the hunger and thirst for God is a most important event in our life. It is the beginning of our salvation.

So much regarding the nature of the hunger that is directed towards holiness. Let us now turn to an examination of the *concept of holiness* itself. In Scripture and in Patristic and other Church writings, God is called *holy* (*hágios*), Angels are called *holy* (*hágioi*), and so are the Righteous. The Church Fathers make it very clear that *God alone is holy by His nature*, whereas the *Angels* and the *Righteous*—the *Saints* in general—*are holy by participation* in the holiness of God. Participation is effected by the Grace of the Holy Spirit. We

---

[1] *Hypotýposis perí Anthrópou*, Athens, 1893, p. 193.

see this strikingly in the account of Pentecost given in the New Testament in the Acts of the Apostles. Here we read that the Apostles "were *filled with the Holy Spirit,*" who appeared to them like tongues of fire (2:3-4). We see this also in St. Paul's Second Epistle to the Thessalonians and in other New Testament texts. St. Paul says: "God hath from the beginning chosen you to salvation through *sanctification* [*hagiasmós*] of the Spirit and belief in the truth" (II Thessalonians 2:13; cf. Romans 15:16, St. Luke 1:35).

In the Septuagint—the Greek language version of the Old Testament—and in the original, Greek-language New Testament, two words with the same root are used to denote holiness: *hagiótes* and *hagiosyne*. *Hagiótes* is used only once in the Old[1] and the New Testaments.[2] *Hagiosyne* appears five times in the Septuagint[3] and three times in the New Testament.[4] Another very important Scriptural term, closely related to these, is *hagiasmós*. This is used ten times in the Old Testament and ten in the New.

The meaning of these three terms is clearer in the New Testament than in the Old. Hence we shall refer chiefly to the New Testament for the ascertainment of their meaning.

Hagiótes, as we noted, appears once in the New Testament. It is used by the Apostle Paul in his Epistle to the Hebrews.

[1] II Maccabees 15:2.
[2] Hebrews 12:10.
[3] Psalms 29:4, 95:6, 96:12, 144:5; II Maccabees 3:12.
[4] Romans 1:4; II Corinthians 7:1; 1 Thessalonians 3:13.

He remarks that God chastens us that we might become *partakers of His holiness* (*metalabeín tes hagiótetos autoú*). From this statement, it is clear that whereas God has holiness by *His nature*, we do not, but have *the possibility of acquiring holiness through participation* in the holiness of God, and that such participation *presupposes purifying discipline.* Saint Paul says: "We have had fathers of our flesh which corrected us... after their own pleasure: but God chastens us for our profit, that we might become partakers of His holiness" (12:9-10).

Hagiosyne, the second Greek word for holiness that was mentioned, similarly denotes both the holiness inherent in God and the holiness of human beings acquired through participation in the holiness of God.

In the Septuagint, the Prophet-King David speaks eloquently of the *hagiosyne* of God. He says: "Sing unto the Lord, O ye saints of His, and give thanks at the remembrance of His holiness" (Psalm 29:4). Again, he says: "Rejoice in the Lord, ye righteous; and give thanks at the remembrance of His holiness" (Psalm 96:12). And again, he says: "They shall speak of the majesty of the glory of Thy holiness" (Psalm 144:5).

These verses show that David views the holiness of God as something *majestic, glorious*, eliciting in him who contemplates it great joy.

Paul, too, speaks of *hagiosyne*. He employs this term in referring to *participated* holiness in humans. Thus, in his Second Epistle to the Corinthians, he says: "Let us cleanse ourselves from all filthiness of flesh and spirit, *perfecting holiness* in the fear of God" (2 Corinthians 7:1). And addressing the Thessalonians, he speaks to them of *establishing* their "hearts unblameable *in holiness* before God" (I Thessalonians 3:13).

The third Greek word that I mentioned, *hagiasmós*, is used to denote *sanctification—the process of becoming holy*. In his Epistle to the Romans, St. Paul exhorts them: "Now yield your [bodily] members servants to righteousness for *sanctification*" (6:19).

According to the teaching of the Apostles and the Church Fathers, Christians become participants in God's holiness through the action or Grace of the Holy Spirit. Participation is *not* in God's *essence* (*ousía*). The essence of God cannot be participated in, known, or contemplated. But we can participate in and experience God's uncreated "energy" (*enérgeia*) or "energies." It is through this participation and direct experience that one can gain knowledge of *what* holiness is and *that* God exists.

Those who rise to the blessed state of experiencing or contemplating richly the holiness of God see it as ineffable *light, glory, beauty*, and feel inexpressible *joy*.

Abba Philemon, one of the great mystics of the Eastern Orthodox Church, who, appears to have lived in the sixth or seventh century and wrote some remarkable texts on the spiritual life, says about such experiences: "Quite ineffable and unutterable are the flashes of Divine Beauty. Words cannot explain, hearing cannot believe. Even if you mention the morning star, or the brightness of the moon, or the light of the sun, all these are lowly for picturing to oneself that glory, and fall very far short in comparison with the True Light.[1]

Sanctification admits of *degrees*. The manifestations of it are many and assume various forms. That described by Abba Philemon occurs in the case of those who are far advanced in the spiritual life and are called mystics. In Holy Scripture and in the writings of the Greek Church Fathers, these manifestations are called "fruits" (*karpoi*). The expression "fruits of the Spirit" is used to denote moral and spiritual *virtues*, such as sobriety, long-suffering, gentleness, faith and love, and *positive states* of the soul, such as peace and joy.[2]

To these kinds of sanctification effected in humans by the Grace of the Holy Spirit, the Church Fathers add *purification* (*katharmós*) *of the soul* from vices, passions, and negative thoughts; *the sanctification of the body*; and the *deification* (*théosis*) of man, that is, union with God.[3] Every working of the Holy Spirit in a person constitutes a union with God, but *theosis* is an all-pervasive union, where God acts as the *Ruler* of a person in all his words, actions, thoughts, and feelings. This is the state to which St. Paul attained, as is testified by the following remark which he makes: "I am crucified with

---

[1] *Philokalia*, Vol. 2, Athens, 1958, p. 251.

[2] Galatians 5:22-23; cf. St. Maximos the Confessor: "He who has attained as far as possible perfection, bears as fruits love, joy, peace, long-suffering" (*Philokalia*, Vol.2, p.70).

[3] Cf. St. Maximos the Confessor: "*Gínetai Theós te methéxei tés theikés cháritos*" (*Philokalia*, Vol.2, p.87).

Christ: nevertheless I live; yet not I, but Christ liveth in me" (Galatians 2:20). And it is the state we hunger for when we say in the Lord's Prayer: "Thy Kingdom come, Thy will be done."

It should be added that the sanctification or perfection of a human being attained even in *theosis* is not complete during this life. It is an "unfinished perfection" (*atélestos teleiótes*), as it is called in the *Ladder of Divine Ascent* by St. John Climacos.[1] Perfection will grow endlessly in the life to come, in Heaven. There, according to great holy Fathers such as Gregory of Nyssa, John Climacos, and Gregory of Mount Sinai, the Saints will never cease to grow in knowledge, in love, in glory.

Sanctification, *hagiasmós*, is a *synergistic, Divine-human* process, as we are taught by Holy Scripture and the Eastern Church Fathers. It is a process in which *God and man cooperate.* Divine help, Divine Grace, comes from the Holy Spirit, *not* as something forced upon man, but *in response* to man's unconstrained will that *asks* and *prays* for it. This fact is implicit in Christ's statement: "Ask, and it shall be given you; seek, and ye shall find; knock, and it shall be opened unto you" (Matthew 7:7).

God has endowed human nature with what the Greek Fathers call *to autexoúsion*—the power of free choice and self-control. And He leaves this power *inviolate.* God is ever

---

[1] *Klimax*, Athens, 1979, Discourse ("Step") 29, par. 3.

ready to bestow upon us His perfecting Grace; but He *waits upon us to ask for it freely, unconstrainedly*. This is taught to us by the Holy Scripture and by the old and the modern Orthodox Saints.

In his already referred to treatise *Concerning Perfection*, St. Gregory of Nyssa tells us that the path to perfection, to holiness, begins with an act of deliberate choice (*eklogé, proaíresis*) of *the higher good* (*to béltion*). Following this choice, one sets out with *zeal to learn how* he may achieve perfection through a life according to virtue.

We can learn this best, he says, from Christ, for "He is the beginning and the ultimate end (*arché kai télos*) of the whole virtuous way of life and of every good lesson. In the next place, we shall learn it by taking as our teacher and guide Paul the Apostle. For he understood with the greatest precision what Christ was, and what a Christian should be like. Paul imitated Christ in a very clear and distinct manner, and transformed his character in accordance with Christ, Who is the original Model (*Protótypon*)."

St. Gregory proposes that each one of us, following the lessons given by our Lord Jesus Christ and Paul the Apostle, and looking to them as to a model, create within ourselves a Christ-like character, as an artist paints a portrait. The artist of this creation (*demiourgía*) will be our deliberate choice; the colors will be the virtues; and our model will be the Archetypal Beauty, that is, the character of Christ.

St. Gregory of Nyssa
Mosaic, Church of Hagia Sophia at Kiev.
Eleventh century.

St. Ephraim the Syrian (306-373)—the greatest of the Syrian Church Fathers—has said something similar, wishing to awaken in his readers the hunger for holiness. "Let us strive," he said, "as if our life were to be painted and placed at a high place, to be exhibited to all. Let us endeavor with zeal to achieve the virtues, in order that nothing blameworthy or unbecoming might appear in the painting depicting our life."[1]

The virtues which will serve as beautiful colors for painting within us a Christian image (*eikón*), St. Gregory of Nyssa tells us, are particularly *humility, gentleness, long-suffering, justice, love*, and *spiritual wisdom*, which has as its beginning the virtue of illuminating *faith*.

In the image that we shall paint within ourselves—that is, in our moral character that we shall create—there shall be no place for vices and passions, such as anger, hatred, malice, and lust. These shall be excluded. For Christ, our Prototype, showed Himself quite free of them.

Having spoken about the nature of hunger and the nature of holiness, I shall now proceed to a discussion of how modern Orthodox Saints can help arouse in us the hunger for holiness and how they teach us the ways of achieving fulfillment of this hunger. The first point to be noted here is this: the fact that modern Orthodox Saints are *closer* to us *in time* makes their example and message find in us more readily a responsive cord. We are so constituted psychologically that recent

---

[1] Ephraim the Syrian, *Asketiká*, translated into modern Greek by Markos D. Sakkorraphos. Athens, 1935, p. 24.

personages seem *more real* than those of the remote past, and their achievements and teaching *more relevant* to us today. This point is developed in a very telling way by St. Nicodemos the Hagiorite in his Introduction to *The New Martyrologion*, which was first published in 1794. This book contains biographies of many Neomartyrs—that is, Saints who suffered Martyrdom since the time of the fall of Constantinople to the Turks (1453).

St. Nicodemos says among other things the following: "These Martyrs are a *renewal* of the whole Orthodox Faith.... Time has this consequence: it renders new things old, and casts old things, after a long duration, into the depths of oblivion, destroys them, and it is as if they had never existed at all." Applying this to the Saints of the remote past on the one hand and to the Neomartyrs on the other, he remarks: "The antiquity of the period during which the early Saints lived, the long time that has intervened from then to the present can cause in some, if not unbelief, at least some doubt or hesitation. One may, that is, wonder how humans, who by nature are weak and timid, endured so many and frightful tortures. But these New Martyrs of Christ, having acted boldly on the recent scene of the world, uproot from the hearts of Christians all doubt and hesitation, and implant or renew in them unhesitating faith in the old Martyrs. Just as new food strengthens all those bodies that are weak from starvation, and just as new rain causes trees that are dried from drought to bloom again, so these New Martyrs strengthen and renew the weak, withered, and old faith of present-day Christians...."

"In addition," continues St. Nicodemos, "these New Martyrs renew in the hearts of today's Christians the teaching [*kérygma*] of the Holy Apostles, confirm the Divine Gospel and the Divinity of Jesus Christ—that He is truly the Son of God, of one essence with the Father and His life-giving Spirit—and proclaim the mystery of the Holy Trinity. In a word, they provide confirmation of the whole Orthodox Faith of Christians. They do this, not with words alone, but rather by means of the most terrible tortures to which they were subjected, by means of their very blood and death."

The substance of what St. Nicodemos says about the relevance of the Neomartyrs to contemporary Orthodox Christians can be said also of the *other* orders of modern Orthodox Saints: Missionaries, Hierarchs, Monastics, and so on. Because of their closeness to us, we take greater interest in the example and message of modern Orthodox Saints than we are likely to take in those Saints who lived a thousand or more years ago, even though their way of life, their spiritual practices and experiences, their character and teaching are essentially the same. Modern Saints admire and imitate the older ones: they follow closely their example, study their teaching carefully, and—what is extremely significant—they confirm it. Those of the modern Saints who write or preach amplify and illustrate the teaching of the older Saints, and relate it to modern realities. Thanks to the modern invention of printing, their teaching has been recorded more fully and can be disseminated far and wide.

In order to *arouse the hunger for holiness* in their fellow Christians, Sts. Macarios of Corinth and Nicodemos the Hagiorite gathered together and prepared for publication many lives of various orders of Saints. In one of the books containing lives of Saints, *The New Eklogion*, Nicodemos stresses the value which reading lives of Saints has for all, whether clergy, monastics, or laity. The lives of Saints, remarks Nicodemos, *offer us excellent examples to be followed and provide sound teaching that is conducive to sanctification.*

The power of *holy icons* to arouse our hunger for holiness and lead to our sanctification has been asserted by these and other modern Saints. St. Nicodemos has made pertinent statements in his works, such as *The Rudder* (*Pedálion*). And St. Nectarios in his *Study Concerning Holy Icons* emphasizes this power of icons. St. Seraphim of Sarov has taught it by his practice of standing before an icon of the Theotokos during his prayers in his cell.

Services in honor of Saints—Akolouthias, as they are called—are conducive to the same end. St. Nicodemos composed or prepared for publication many *Akolouthias*. So also did St. Nikephoros of Chios, who was a younger contemporary of Nicodemos. Nikephoros gathered together many lives of Saints, old and new, some written by himself, and many *Akolouthias* composed by himself, and published them in a large book, to which he gave the title *Neon Leimonárion* ("New Spiritual Meadows").

Sacred poetry in the form of *Akolouthias*, when properly chanted in churches, has a powerful uplifting effect. It arouses in the faithful the hunger for holiness by exhibiting the beauty of holiness in the life and character of the Saints whose memory is being celebrated.

Akolouthias belong to the category of *liturgical* poetry: they are designed to be chanted in church. There is another kind of sacred poetry, intended to be read or recited in private prayer. Both types of sacred poetry are calculated to increase our longing for holiness and to draw fulfilling, sanctifying Divine Grace. St. Nectarios composed poetry of the second type. His most remarkable poetic collection is entitled *Triadikon, or Odes and Hymns to the Triune God*. These odes and hymns are presented as prayers to God, forms of praise of Him, ways of inciting the reader of them to lead a godly life, means of being sanctified. I shall quote two stanzas addressed to the Holy Trinity that are especially relevant to the topic of this discourse:

> Thou Who dost will mercy, have mercy upon
> Those who with faith take refuge in Thee.
> Grant forgiveness of their offences,
> And deliver them from passions and dangers.

> In the ineffable sea of Thy goodness,
> Bestow upon me the light-giving splendor
> Of Thy Divine effulgence, O eternal,
> Light-giving, spiritual Sun.

From our discussion of the relevance of modern Orthodox Saints, it is evident that in various ways they contribute to evoking in us today the hunger for holiness and instructing us in the ways and means of satisfying this, hunger, of becoming holy.

THE PROPHET-KING MOSES
Fresco in a side chapel of the Monastery of
Vatopedi at Mount Athos.

CHAPTER TWO

Striving for Holiness*

This talk will be focused on the *various means* that according to Orthodox Christian teaching are to be used in one's endeavor *to become holy.* Before proceeding to discuss such means, it is proper to answer two questions. The first question is this: *Why* should we strive *to become holy?* The second question is: *What is holiness,* which we should strive to acquire? Or, putting it differently, *what constitutes our being holy?*

The answer to the first question is to be found in Holy Scripture and is amplified in the writings of the holy Fathers of the Church. In the Old Testament God tells the Prophet Moses

* A lecture sponsored by the Orthodox Church of America, Diocese of the South, at its Twenty-first Diocesan Assembly held in Miami, Florida, July 7-9, 1998, and delivered on July 9 at the hall of the Orthodox Cathedral of Christ the Savior, in the presence of the Most Reverend Archbishop Dimitri of Dallas, Texas.

and his brother Aaron: "Ye shall therefore *sanctify* yourselves, and ye shall be *holy*, for I am *holy*." This statement appears in the *Book of Leviticus* (11:44). Moses and Aaron are asked to convey it to their people. God repeats this statement twice in *Leviticus*. In Chapter 19, we read: "And the Lord spoke unto Moses, saying: "Speak unto all the congregation of the children of Israel, and say unto them: *"Ye shall be holy*, for I the Lord your God am holy" (19:1-2). And in the next chapter of *Leviticus* there is the following statement: *"Sanctifies yourselves* therefore, and *be ye holy*, for I am the Lord your God. And ye shall keep my commandments (*prostágmata*) and do them: *I am the Lord Who sanctifies you*" (20:7-8).

In these passages God is telling the Old Testament people *to sanctify themselves*, that is, *to become holy* (*ésesthe hágioi*). The import of these passages is not to be taken as being restricted to the Old Testament people. They are to be taken as applying to *all peoples* of *all places* and of *all times*. God says that He Himself is holy and wants all to become themselves holy.

Thus, the answer to the question *why* we should strive to become holy is given in the Old Testament by God Himself: it is *man's destiny willed by God Himself*. This destiny is *the highest conceivable*.

Although lofty, it is a goal that *is attainable*. For God, being *all-good and all-wise*, would not have ordained for us something impossible.

When we turn to the *New Testament* we find the same answer, couched in different terms and given by the God-Man,

Jesus Christ. In the Sermon on the Mount Christ says: "Be ye therefore *perfect*, as your Father Who is in Heaven is perfect" (Matthew, 5:48). The term "perfect" (*téleios*) is used here instead of the word "holy" (*hágios*). In the *Old Testament* passages that I quoted, God calls Himself "holy" (*hágios*); in the New Testament, God the Father is said to by Christ to be "perfect" (*téleios*). And He asks His disciples to strive to become "perfect," as God the Father is "perfect."

Like the *Old Testament* statement, "Sanctify yourselves," Christ's statement to His disciples "Be ye therefore perfect," is to be taken as applying to *all* men of *all* times. And the terms "holy" and "perfect" are to be taken as *synonyms*. This is a point I shall discuss at some length in my answer to the second question, to which we now turn.

The question is: *What is holiness*, which we should strive to acquire? Or, putting it differently, *What constitutes our being holy or perfect?* Before attempting to answer this question, it is necessary that I emphasize that God *is holy*, and *has always been holy*, whereas we human beings *have to become holy*. How? Through our *striving and Divine Grace*. This is manifest in the already quoted passages of the book of *Leviticus* and the Sermon on the Mount. In *Leviticus* the Lord says of Himself: "I *am* holy;" whereas to the people He says: "Ye *shall* sanctify yourselves, and ye *shall be* holy." And Christ says: "*Be* ye therefore *perfect*, as your Father Who is in heaven *is perfect.*" Here, "*be* perfect" means "*become* perfect."

As to the *nature of holiness*, we have to collate various passages in Holy Scripture in order to form an idea as *what* it is. We have to confirm that the terms *holiness*, used in the *Old Testament* passages that I have quoted, and the term *perfection* used in the *New Testament*, are indeed employed as equivalent terms denoting the *same* reality.

The identity of the *meaning* of the words is implied by the following. In the same Gospel in which our Lord exhorts his disciples to strive *to become perfect*, He advises a young man *what to do* in order to become perfect, saying: "If thou wilt be perfect, go and sell that thou hast, and give to the poor, and thou shalt have treasure in heaven: and come and follow me" (Matthew 19:21).

Proceeding to the *Epistles* of St. Paul the Apostle, we note that in speaking of the *ultimate goal* of our striving sometimes he speaks of it as being *holiness* and at other times as being *perfection*. In other words, Paul uses these two words interchangeably, as denoting the same thing. Thus, in his *Epistle to the Romans*, he says: "Now being made free from sin, and become servants of God, ye have your fruit unto *sanctification (hagiasmós)*, and the end everlasting life" (Romans 6:22). Similarly, in the *First Epistle to the Thessalonians* he says: "For this is the will of God, your sanctification (4: 3): for God hath not called us unto uncleanness, but unto *holiness*" (4:7). In other Epistles, he employs the term *perfection* instead of holiness. Thus, he says in the *Epistle to the Ephesians*: "He (Christ) gave some, apostles; and some, prophets; and some evangelists; and some, pastors and teachers; for the *perfecting* of the saints, ...till we all come to the unity of the faith, and the knowledge of the Son of God, unto a *perfect* man, unto the measure of the stature of the fullness

ST. PAUL THE APOSTLE
Detail of a panel icon by Andrei Rublev.
Early fifteenth century.

of Christ" (4:11-13). Similarly, in his *Epistle to the Colossians*, Paul says: "We preach Christ, warning every man, and teaching every man in all wisdom; that we may present every man *perfect* in Christ Jesus" (1:28; cf. 4:12).

The term *perfection* as denoting the highest, ultimate goal of human striving, appears also in the Epistle of James the Apostle. He remarks: "Let patience have her perfect work, that ye may be perfect and entire, wanting nothing" (1:4; cf.3:2).

There are other passages in the *New Testament* that could be quoted for establishing the identity of the meaning of the words holiness and perfection, as signifying the same ultimate goal which God has ordained for human beings. But those just quoted should suffice.

It is to be noted that this identity of meaning of the terms holiness and perfection is implicit also in the *Old Testament*. Thus, while in *Leviticus* the exhortation is that we become *holy*, in *Deuteronomy* it is that we become *perfect*. In Chapter 18 of *Deuteronomy* we read: "Thou shalt be perfect with the Lord thy God" (18:13).

Thus, the call to holiness (*hagiótes*) is a call to perfection (*teleiótes*). But in *what* does man's perfection consist? According to the holy Orthodox Church Fathers it consists in the attainment of (1) *purity*, (2) *likeness to God*, and (3) *union with Him*, called *theosis, deification*.

Purity consists in freedom from *passions* and *vices*, while *likeness* consists in the attainment of all the *virtues* or excellences of the soul. *Theosis* means union with God—with His *energies*, not with God's *essence*. It is possible for an individual to *participate* in the *energies* of God but *not* in His *essence*. God's essence (*ousia*) is wholly inaccessible to us. It cannot be known, contemplated, or participated in. Through participation and direct experience of God's *energies* one can gain knowledge *that He exists* and *what His holiness is*.

God's holiness is *preeminently* experienced or contemplated as *ineffable light, glory, beauty,* and *blessedness*. Those who experience it in this way are called *mystics*. They are persons far advanced in the spiritual life. Others experience God's holiness as invisible Grace that *strengthens* them in situations of temptation, in their struggle to achieve purity and to grow in the virtues.

We will turn now to a question, an answer to which will constitute the rest of my talk. The question is: "*How* should we *strive* to become holy? What are the *acts*, the *practices* that we should perform in order to become holy?

First of all, we must perform an *act of choice*, freely, without any constraint by anyone, *to take the path* that leads to the attainment of holiness or spiritual perfection.

This act of choice must be followed by a *firm resolve to tread that path*. Then one must study the lives of saints and *use them as models*. St. Basil the Great has this to say about such studies:

"Just as painters in working from models constantly gaze at their exemplar and thus strive to transfer the expression of the original to their own artistry, so too he who is anxious to make himself perfect in all kinds of virtue must gaze upon the lives of the saints as upon statues, so to speak, that move and act, and must make their excellence his own by imitation."

The treatise *Concerning Perfection* of St. Gregory of Nyssa, who was a brother of St. Basil, will be found very helpful by spiritual strivers. Gregory uses his brother's idea of having an *exemplar* (*protótypon*) and he elaborates on it.[1]

From reading many lives of saints written by pious Orthodox writers, whose aim is not to entertain, or merely to provide information, but to *edify*, one can learn a great deal about *the way to holiness*. Each serious reader is likely to find among the various saints his favorite one. But we should avoid exclusiveness. We should learn something of real value to us from the life and sayings of every saint that we study.

St. Athanasios' *Life of St. Antony* is very instructive in this connection. He says that St. Antony the Great visited *many* spiritual men and learned something important from *each one* of them. "He learned thoroughly where each surpassed him in zeal and discipline. He observed the graciousness of one; the unceasing prayer of another. He took knowledge of freedom from anger of one; of another's loving kindness, and still another's fasting and sleeping on the ground. He watched carefully the meekness of one and the forbearance of another. He took note of the piety towards Christ and mutual love that animated all. Thus filled, St. Antony returned to his own place of spiritual practice, and henceforth would strive to *unite* the good qualities of each, and was eager to acquire himself the virtues of all."

At the beginning of this quotation, Athanasios mentions St. Antony's *zeal* or *fervor*. We are told that he learned thoroughly where each one surpassed him in *zeal*." This spurred

[1] *Op. cit.*, 235M ff.

him to increase his own zeal in various practices of discipline or *askesis*. This is an important point. For without zeal one cannot make significant progress. The importance of zeal in the spiritual life was emphasized by the Apostle Paul. Thus, in his First Epistle to the Corinthians he says: "Covet zealously the best spiritual gifts."[1]

Lack of zeal or fervor means lack of love for God, since the path is directed to the attainment of *likeness to God* and *union with Him*. Such lack means ignoring the first and great commandment of God, which states: "Thou shalt love the Lord thy God with all thy heart, and with all thy soul, and with all thy mind" (Matthew 22:37, Mark 12:30, Luke 10:27). God must be given *first* place in our lives. To give Him the second place is to give Him no place at all, as the great Russian poet Pushkin (19th century) remarked.

Our zeal must begin at the time of our *free choice and firm resolve* to enter the path that leads to holiness and continue without interruption until the time of our departure from the earth. This choice and resolve is called by St. John Climacos "the violent renunciation of the vain way of life." He places it as the *first step* in the thirty-step *Ladder of Divine Ascent*.

It must be emphasized that of crucial importance for success in the path of holiness, besides our free choice, firm resolve, and spiritual zeal, is *divine help*. Our Lord Jesus Christ said: "Without Me ye can do nothing" (John 15:5). He also said: "Ask and it shall be given you" (Matthew 7:7); and "He that abideth in Me, and I in him, the same bringeth forth much fruit" (John 15:5).

[1] 1 Corinthians 12:31; cf. 1 Corinthians 14:1, and Galatians 4:18.

In his *Diary of a Writer*, Dostoievsky calls striving for spiritual development "work upon oneself." He explains that this consists in *self-imposed, relentless, uninterrupted self-discipline*. Contemporary thinkers, he remarks, reject such discipline. However, he observes, it is necessary if we are to mould ourselves into *true human beings*.[1] This passage emphasizes the points I just mentioned.

What Dostoievsky calls "self-discipline" is called by the Greek Church Fathers *askesis*. This word means *exercise, practice, training*. The noun "askesis" does not appear in the *New Testament*, but the verb form of the term is used by St. Paul in the *Acts of the Apostles*. In Chapter 14, he says: "Herein do I *exercise* (*askó*) myself, to have always a conscience void of offence towards God and men" (24:16).

An equivalent verb appears in the *Gospel according to Luke* and in the Epistles of St. Paul: *agonízomai*, which means *I strive, I struggle, I exert myself*. In the *Gospel*, Christ, in speaking of the Kingdom of God, tells people: "*Strive* (*agonízesthe*) to enter in at the narrow gate" (13:24). The same word appears in Paul's Epistles. In the *First Epistle to the Corinthians*, comparing the spiritual striver to an athlete who is training for a contest, hoping to win the prize, Paul says: "Every man that *striveth* for the mastery exercises self-restraint in all things. The athletes do it to obtain a perishable crown; but we an imperishable one" (9:25). In his *Epistle to the Colossians* he says: "I toil, *striving with energy* which Christ mightily inspires within me" (1:29; cf. 4:12). In his *First Epistle to Timothy* he exhorts this disciple with these

[1] *Diary of a Writer*, London, 1949, pp. 604-605.

FYODOR DOSTOIEVSKY (1821-1881)
Portrait by Pièrov (1872)

words: "*Strive in the good struggle* of the Faith, lay hold of the eternal life" (6:12). And in the *Second Epistle to Timothy* he says: "I have *exerted* myself in the good struggle, I have finished the race, I have kept the Faith" (4:7).

The Apostle Paul also employs the noun *struggle* (*agón*) several times in his Epistles in speaking of what the Church Fathers later called *askesis*. He does not explain the nature of the "struggle," except incidentally and partially, in one of the passages that I have quoted, where he speaks of *self-restraint* (*engráteia*) in all things. A fuller idea of what he means by "struggle" or "striving" can be acquired by going over *all* his Epistles. Scattered in them are references to *fasting, watch-fulness, unceasing prayer, chastity, patience* in all things, and *control of the tongue.* Chapter 6 of his *Epistle to the Colossians* is particularly enlightening on this subject.

I have called attention to the fact that Christ uses the word "strive" in His exhortation: "Strive to enter the Kingdom of God through the narrow gate." What He means is apparent from His example and teaching. It means fasting, prayer, inner watchfulness, longsuffering, loving God and our fellow men. Christ fasted during a period of forty days and nights, thus offering an example of the importance of fasting. He also instructed people how to behave when fasting. He prayed at the Mount of Olives, and thus offered a lesson on the importance of prayer; and he often spoke on the need of prayer and gave a model prayer to be recited, called "The Lord's Prayer" (Matthew 6:9-13). All these things and others He did in order to teach mankind how to strive for holiness.

Following faithfully the teaching that has been offered by word and example by our Lord Jesus Christ and His Apostles, most notably the Apostle Paul, the holy Fathers of the Church *lived* this teaching and attained thereby an illuminated state of mind. Precious fruits of this have been the writings which they authored. These, taken together with the Holy Scriptures, constitute an all-encompassing body of Christian instruction. We gain access to this teaching by the practice of reading the Scriptures, especially the *New Testament*, the lives of saints, and Patristic writings, particularly works such as the *Ladder of Divine Ascent* by St. John Climacos, the *Evergetinos*, and the *Philokalia*.

Regular reading of the Holy Scriptures and of works such as those that I just mentioned increasingly frees us from our first, greatest enemy in the spiritual life, namely, *ignorance* of the Faith. Such reading will also free us from our second great enemy: *forgetfulness* of the teachings of the Faith, as well as from our third great enemy: *lack of zeal.*

These teachings constitute *Christian wisdom*—wisdom that pertains to the spiritual life. Our assimilation of this wisdom constitutes the Christian virtue of wisdom, which is the fountainhead of the other virtues, including *hope* and *love*. Without Christian faith or Christian wisdom there is neither Christian hope nor Christian love.

About my use here of the word *wisdom*, it is to be noted that readings in church from Holy Scripture are preceded by the priest's saying aloud: "Wisdom." Thus, at the Divine Liturgy, before the Apostolic reading, and then before the reading of the Gospel excerpt, the priest says to the congregation: "Wisdom" (*Sophia*). He does the same before the Old Testament readings

The value of reading the Scriptures is emphasized both by Christ and by St. Paul. Christ says: "Search the Scriptures, for in them ye think ye have eternal life; and it is they which testify of Me" (John 5: 39). And Paul says: "All Scripture is inspired by God, and is profitable for teaching, for correction, for instruction in righteousness: that the man of God may be perfect, thoroughly furnished unto all good works" (2 Timothy 3:16-17).

St. Isaac the Syrian makes a similar remark in one of his Ascetic Discourses. He says: "The continual study of Holy Scripture is the light of the soul. It brings to the soul profitable memories—those of being on our guard with regard to the passions, of abiding in the longing for God, and purity of prayer."[1] In like vein, another great Syrian saint, Ephraim the Syrian, remarks: "Studying the words of God nourishes the soul, protects and disciplines the body, and drives demons away."[2]

The great mystic Symeon the New Theologian (11th century), tells us: "Those things which are read in *the writings of the saints* illuminate the mind, sanctify the soul, and through it transmit sanctification to the body, and make it healthier and stronger."[3]

---

[1] *Ta Heurethénta Asketiká* ("The Discovered Ascetic Discourses"), edited by Nikephoros Theotokis, Athens, 1895 (1st edition, Leipzig, 1770), Discourse 33, p. 141.

[2] *Ephraim tou Syrou ta Asketiká* ("The Ascetic Discourses of Ephraim the Syrian"), translated into the vernacular by Markos D. Sakkorraphos, Athens, 1935, p.14).

[3] *Tou Hosíou Symeón tou Néou Theológou ta Heuriskómena* ("The Extant Works of Saint Symeon the New Theologian"), Syros, 1886, p. 415.

Speaking more broadly, following the sacred tradition of the Orthodox Church, we may say that whoever reads the books of the *Prophets*, the *Apostles*, the *Evangelists*, the *lives of Saints*, and the *discourses and sayings of the holy Fathers*, and does so attentively, meditatively, and prayerfully in order to know the will of God, such a person attracts the grace of God to himself, and that grace strengthens him to do what he has learned from such reading.

Psalmody or *chanting*, which is a combination of vocal *reading and prayer*, is another practice to be used by the striver. This practice is taught both by Holy Scripture and by the great Church Fathers. In the Gospels, we read that after the Mystical Supper, Christ and His disciples "sang a hymn" and went with Him to the Mount of Olives (Matthew 26:30; Mark 14:26). St. Paul, writing to the Ephesians, tells them: "Sing and psalmodize to the Lord in your heart, always and for everything giving thanks in the name of our Lord Jesus Christ" (Ephesians 5:19-20). Again, writing to the Colossians, he tells them to thank God by singing "Psalms and hymns and spiritual songs" (Colossians, 3:16). And again, in the *Acts of the Apostles*, he and Silas are said to have prayed and sang hymns to God while in prison (16:25).

In the writings of the Church Fathers, especially in those gathered in the *Philokalia*, psalmody is often mentioned as a part of askesis. Its value is duly emphasized. St. John Chrysostom says: "Nothing uplifts the soul so much, and gives it wings, and frees it from worldly cares, so much as divine song.... This gives it at once both pleasure and benefit."[1] Other

[1] *Patrologia Graeca*, Vol. 55, 156-157A.

Fathers, such as St. John Climacos, emphasize the value of chanting in purifying the soul of specific passions, such as *anger, despondency,* and *sorrow*, which have a bad influence on both the soul and the body.

These three passions are not the only ones from which the striver for holiness must free himself. St. John Cassian the Roman (fl. 430) lists *eight* chief passions: (1) gluttony, (2) lust, (3) avarice, (4) anger, (5) sorrow, (6) despondency, (7) vanity, and (8) pride. He devotes a whole treatise to them, explaining the nature of each one and how we are to free ourselves from them. The text is contained in the first volume of the *Philokalia*. St. John Climacos, too, discusses them at length in his *Ladder of Divine Ascent*. He explains their nature and the means whereby we can oppose them and uproot them.

The means emphasized in Holy Scripture and the writings of the holy Fathers are *general self-restraint, fasting, attention or watchfulness, and prayer*. Through *self-restraint* with respect to food and drink—the avoidance of excesses—and the observance of the fasts ordained by the Church, gluttony and lust are effectively overcome. St. John Climacos remarks characteristically: "Satiety in food is the father of fornication (*porneía*); but restraint of the stomach is an agent of purity (*hagneía*)."[1]

With regard to *fasting*, Meletios Pegas (16th century), Patriarch of Alexandria, says this in his book *Fount of Gold*: "The mind (*nous*) is divinized through fasting, and the flesh

---

[1] *Klimax*, Athens, 1979, Discourse 14:3; *The Ladder of Divine Ascent*, Boston, 1991, Step 14:5.

is spiritualized through fasting.... As far as it is susceptible, the mind is deified and comes to be with God. Fasting and prayer are divine weapons. They deaden the passions, vanquish the enemy (Satan) and are conducive to the Kingdom Heaven."[1]

Fasting is ordained by the Church on Wednesdays and Fridays, during the Great Lent, the first two weeks of August, and on certain other days. It consists in the following: (1) *Reduction* of the quantity of food eaten; (2) *abstention* from foods of animal origin, namely meat, fish, eggs, milk, cheese, butter and other dairy products, as well as from "gourmet dishes" designed for sensual gratification and from alcoholic drinks.

Such fasting should be accompanied, according to the teaching of the Church, by *mental fasting*. This consists in the avoidance of unnecessary talking, slander, and hatred; the curbing of other passions; and the avoidance of bad and useless thoughts. "Passions" are bad thoughts, impure thoughts, charged with emotion. If they are not opposed and gradually banished from our life, passions became *vices*, fixed traits of character, second nature. "Passions" are *incipient* forms of diseases of the soul, while vices are *advanced* forms of diseases of the soul. It is much more difficult to free oneself from vices than it is from passions. Great struggle is needed, accompanied by heartfelt prayers. Those who do not free themselves from passions and vices remain to the end of their lives sick in soul. Thus they exclude themselves from the Kingdom of God. Referring to such individual, St. Paul says

[1] *Chrysopegé*, ed, by G. Valetas, Athens, 1958, pp.93-94.

that "neither fornicators, nor idolaters, nor adulterers, nor effeminate, nor homosexuals, nor thieves, nor covetous, nor drunkards, nor revilers, nor extortioners shall inherit the Kingdom of God" (1 Corinthians 6:9)

An extremely important means of preventing passions and vices is the practice of *guarding the five senses, the imagination, the mind, and the "heart."* This is a vast subject. St. Nicodemos the Hagiorite (1749-1809) devoted a whole book to it, entitled *Handbook of Counsel.*[1] First printed in Vienna in 1801, an English translation of this important and authoritative work was published in New York in 1989 with the title *A Handbook of Spiritual Counsel.*

The subject was not as difficult to treat in St. Nicodemos' time as it is today. The "mass media of communication" did not exist then: the radio, television, daily newspapers, magazines, audio- and video-cassettes. Today people are constantly bombarded from all directions by soul-defiling sights and sounds. Few persons are aware of the vital importance of guarding their senses of sight and hearing from this continuous assault by day and night. Entering through our eyes and ears, it promotes the growth in us of all kinds of passions, and thereby of vices and resultant evil actions. For we become like that which we habitually contemplate.[2]

In his *Epistle to the Philippians*, Paul the Apostle makes a statement that sums up what things we should *allow* to enter our senses of sight and hearing and thereby our soul: "Whatsoever things are true, whatsoever things are honest, whatsoever things are just, whatsoever things are pure, what-

---

[1] *Symbouleutikón Encheirídion.*
[2] See my book *Fine Arts as Therapy*, Belmont, MA, 1998, pp. 47-49.

soever things are lovely, whatsoever things are of good report; if there be any virtue and if there be any praise" (4:8).

Such objects are rarely presented by the mass media of communication to our sight and hearing. The passion called gluttony, which involves the sense of taste, is nurtured into greatness by these media by presenting pictures and praises of various tasty foods and drinks, usually not health promoting ones. The sense of smell is corrupted and health is undermined by the practice of smoking, a practice that is encouraged by clever advertisements. The passion of smoking has no place in the life of the striver for holiness. For with the destruction of health little spiritual progress can be made. We might recall here the statement of Paul: "Know ye not that ye are the temple of God? If any man defile the temple of God, him shall God destroy; for the temple of God is holy, which temple ye are" (1 Corinthians 3:16-17).[1]

The path to holiness is obviously a *holistic* one, involving the whole man, the soul and the body. It calls for and leads to the purification of both.

The first great stage of attainment in this path is freedom from passions and their resultant vices. It is called "passionlessness" and "purity." The notions of *inner purification* and *inner purity* appear, often in the New Testament. In the Sermon the Mount Christ says: "Blessed are the pure in heart, for they shall see God" (Matthew 5:8). In Chapter 23 of the Gospel according to Matthew, addressing the Scribes and the Pharisees, Christ criticizes them for busying them-

[1] For a comprehensive discussion of the evil effects of smoking on the body and the soul see my monograph *Smoking and the Orthodox Christian,* C.T.O.S., Etna, California, 1992.

selves with *outer* purity and failing to strive for *inner* purity: "Ye make clean," He says, "the outside of the cup and of the platter, but inside they are full of extortion and injustice" (23:25). And He advises them: "Cleanse first that which is within the cup and the platter" (23:26; cf. Luke 11:39-40). St. Paul also emphasizes the need of our purifying ourselves of all defiling emotions and desires. He says: "Let us cleanse ourselves of all filthiness of flesh and spirit, perfecting holiness" (2 Corinthians 7:1).

What is the "filthiness" of which we must cleanse ourselves and thus "perfect holiness" within us? Christ gives the answer. He cites as examples of things that defile us "evil thoughts, murders, adulteries, fornications, thefts, false witness, blasphemies" (Matthew 15:19). In other words, states which the holy Church Fathers call passions and vices.

From the already quoted passage in the Sermon on the Mount, it is evident that passionlessness, or purity from passions and vices, links man to God, the fount of holiness: "Blessed are the pure in heart, for they shall see God" (Matthew 5:8).

Another integral part of holiness is *the presence of the virtues* in a person. The virtues are excellences, beautiful traits of character, manifested in beautiful practices. The possession of the virtues, which are coexistent with purity, render one a *likeness of God*. This is aptly expressed by the following statement in the *Ladder of Divine Ascent*: "The firmament has the stars for its beauty, and freedom from the passions has the virtues for its adornment."[1]

---

[1] Discourse or Step 29, par. 1: English edition, Step 29, par. 2.

Prominent among the virtues are *faith, hope*, and *love*, and the four "most general virtues" of *wisdom, courage, temperance,* and *justice*. Besides these, often mentioned and emphasized in Holy Scripture and Patristic writings, are *humility, longsuffering,* and *gentleness*.

The practices that are conducive to the acquisition of these virtues are many. Some are bodily, others are spiritual. Among the bodily are fasting, reading, chanting, prostrations, standing at prayer, and silence, or the avoidance of all unnecessary talking. Among the mental or spiritual practices are inner attention or watchfulness, prayer, and regular participation in the sacramental life of the Church.

About the various practices, St. Seraphim of Sarov (1759-1833) says: "Every good work—fasting, vigils, prayers, almsgiving, and all good deeds done for the sake of Christ—give us the perfecting Grace of the Holy Spirit of God. But prayer provides it most of all. For it is always at hand and is possible for everyone: rich and poor, noble and lowly, strong and weak, healthy and sick, righteous and sinful.... More than anything else, it brings with it the Spirit of God."[1]

St. Nicodemos the Hagiorite emphasizes the surpassing value of mental prayer in the path to holiness and union with God. This prayer, also known as the "Jesus Prayer," consists in repeating mentally, with the mind drawn into what Scripture and the Church Fathers call the "heart," the following words: "Lord Jesus Christ, Son of God, have mercy upon me." In his *Handbook of Counsel*, Nicodemos says that this

---

[1] Quoted from Vol. 5 of my series *Modern Orthodox Saints*, entitled *St. Seraphim of Sarov*, pp. 98-99.

prayer is "laborious and effortful, yet it is correspondingly fruitful, being the chiefest, and highest activity of the mind. For it unites the mind with God. It purifies the mind more than all the algebras, physics, metaphysics, and all the other sciences of secular learning. It renders man spiritual and a contemplator of God."[1]

St. Cosmas Aitolos (1714-1779) has spoken eloquently and emphatically about the importance of participating regularly in the services of the Church. In one of his sermons he says the following: "Do not separate yourselves from Christ and the church. Go to church to listen attentively to the Orthros. Similarly, attend the Divine Liturgy.... Whoever, my Brethren, hears the bells of the church and is slothful to go to church shall be drowned in sin. The priest is the herald of the Ark. The church is an Ark. Those brethren who worship in church will be forgiven their sins and they will not be drowned by their faults."[2]

In the process of striving for victory over the passions and vices and the acquisition of the virtues, the virtues continuously grow and render us more and more "in the likeness of God." According to the Orthodox teaching, all men are "in the image of God," because all have a soul that possesses the faculty of reason and that of free choice and self-control, and is endowed with immortality; but only those are "in the likeness of God" who have achieved victory over the passions and vices and have acquired all the virtues.

[1] *Symbouleutikón Encheirídion*, 2nd ed., Athens, 1886, pp. 116-117.
[2] Quoted from my book *St. Cosmas Aitolos*, 2nd ed. 1975, pp. 71-72. See Augoustinos Kantiotis, *Ho Hágios Kosmás ho Aitolós*, 3rd ed., Athens, 1966, pp. 281-282.

When an individual has attained to the state of purity and likeness to God, "while still in the flesh," as St. John Climacos remarks, "he has God dwelling within him as his ruler in all his words, and deeds, and thoughts, and through illumination he apprehends the will of God as a sort of inner voice, and becomes superior to every human teaching. 'He no longer lives himself, but Christ lives in him,' as he[1] who fought the good fight, finished the course, and kept the Faith, says."[2]

Very high as this level of holiness or spiritual perfection is, it is not the ultimate limit of man's spiritual perfection. St. John Climacos speaks of "the unfinished perfection of the perfect (*he teleía ton teleíon atélestos teleiótes*)."[3] And St. Symeon the New Theologian says in this connection the following: "Through a clear revelation from Above the saints know that in fact their perfection is endless, their progress in glory will be eternal, that in them there will be a continual increase in Divine radiance, and that an end to their progress will never occur."[4]

Similar statements appear in the *Ladder of Divine Ascent*, in the treatise *Concerning Perfection* of St. Gregory of Nyssa, in the *Philokalia*, and in other Patristic writings. Such passages are quite in accord with the statement, of our Lord Jesus Christ that "Whosoever hath shall be given, and he shall have more abundance."[5]

---

[1] The reference is to St. Paul in the *Epistle to the Galatians* 2:20, and to his *Second Epistle to Timothy* 4:7.
[2] *Klimax*, Athens, 1979, Discourse 29, p. 166, par, 15.
[3] *Ibid.*, p. 165, par 3.
[4] *The Extant Works of Saint Symeon the New Theologian*, Part Two, p. 41.
[5] Matthew 13:12, 25:29; Mark 4:25; Luke 8:18, 19:26.

ST. NECTARIOS OF AEGINA
(1846-1920)
Panel icon by Photios Kontoglou.

CHAPTER THREE

St. Nectarios' Counsels for Spiritual Strivers*

In 1904, while serving as Director of the Rizarios Ecclesi-astical School for training priests located in Athens, St. Nectarios founded the Holy Trinity Convent on the island of Aegina (near Piraeus). The occasion for establishing it was provided by some pious women who used to go to him for Confession and to receive his spiritual counsel. They often expressed to him their desire to embrace the monastic life, so he built Holy Trinity Convent and sent the women there.

In 1908, he retired from the Rizarios School and withdrew to the Convent. There he served as its priest, spiritual guide, and confessor. During the four-year interim period—1904 to 1908—he used to send to them from time to time letters of counsel.

* Lecture delivered in May, 1995, at Holy Cross Greek Orthodox School of Theology in Brookline, Massachusetts, at a seminar course on St. Nectarios directed by Professor Cleopas Strongyllis, Archimandrite, and attended by the students of the graduating class.

The noted Athonite monk Theocletos Dionysiatis, a disciple of the blessed Elder Gabriel Dionysiatis, published in 1979 thirty-five of these letters in his book *Saint Nectarios of Aegina*.[1] Recently, these letters were published by him in separate book form, under the title *35 Pastoral Epistles*.[2] Scattered throughout the letters are many valuable spiritual counsels. Although these are addressed to monastics, every spiritual striver will find them applicable also to himself.

The first important counsel that appears in this collection of letters pertains to *the practice of Christian love*. St. Nectarios introduces his counsel on this subject by saying that God created man "in His image" in order to render us partakers of His goodness. Dwelling on the significance of the phrase "in the image of God," Nectarios says that this implies that love for God and neighbor is *innate* in our heart. It is the first law of Christian ethics.

Our love for God, he counsels, following Christ's teaching, must be with our whole soul, with our whole heart, with all our strength, and with all our mind; and our love for our neighbor must be similar to our love for ourselves.

From this innate law of love spring, according to our Saint, the laws of love of *the beautiful, the good, the true,* and *the just.* Consequently, he continues, in order for a person to make progress spiritually and to become a partaker of Divine goodness and blessedness, he must observe these laws of love.

The observance of these laws, remarks St. Nectarios, is directly related to *conscience* (*syneídesis*). This important

[1] *Ho Hágios Nektários Aegínes.*
[2] *35 Poimantikés Epistolés.*

faculty prompts us to observe with strictness the Commandments of God. Whether we do so or not is ascertained by *self-examination.*[1] For this reason, he advises the practice of *daily self-examination.* He says:

"Examine your heart and discover its moral state. Does it *condemn you* for the transgression of moral laws? Does it *protest* because you suppress it? Does it *censure* you for having neglected your *duties?* Do you observe in your heart any *vices, faults, passions,* or *bad thoughts?*"

With regard to *duties*, St. Nectarios distinguishes three kinds: (1) duties to God, (2) duties to our neighbor, and (3) duties to ourselves. Our duties to God are to observe His Commandments, to thank Him, and to glorify Him. Our duties to our neighbor are to love him as we love ourselves, to forgive him when he does something unjust to us, and to pray for him. Our duties to our self are to take care for the health of both our soul and our body.

Concerning *vices*, he especially emphasizes the need of *struggle* to uproot *pride* from our soul. "Let our work be the searching of our heart lest there lies hidden in it pride, like a poisonous snake." Pride, he says, is a vice that gives birth to many other vices. It poisons and deadens every virtue. For this reason one should watch lest this poisonous serpent be in his heart.

This self-examination, he goes on to say, must be carried on *unceasingly*, day and night. For like a serpent, pride lurks everywhere and poisons everything. We must *search* for it

---

[1] For an extensive discussion on conscience see Chapter III of my book *Byzantine Thought and Art*, Belmont, MA, 1968 and later editions, pp. 40-47.

and for the vices that spring from it. We must *oppose* it and *banish* it. If we succeed in freeing ourselves from pride and acquiring the virtue that is opposed to it, namely, *humility*, and enthroning humility in our heart, "we have everything." The reason for this is the fact that humility brings with it all the other virtues. Humility has been characterized as "elevating," because together all the virtues elevate the soul "from earth to Heaven."

St. Nectarios concludes his counsel regarding the vice of pride and the virtue of humility by saying: *Love* humility, struggle to *acquire* it, and *enthrone* it within your heart.

In some of his letters the Saint discusses *egoism*. He analyzes it, characterizes it as a terrible disease of the soul, and stresses the need of struggling against it and uprooting it. Egoism is clearly an aspect of pride. It manifests itself as *disobedience, self-complacency, grumbling, vanity, ambition*, and the like.

The uprooting of egoism is, he says, "*the first step* of virtue. Without this victory no success in goodness is possible." A mighty struggle is necessary for this, because egoism is like the many-headed Hydra of ancient Greek mythology. For if one cut off one head of this monster, another head of another form grew. And he explains: "Although we succeed in withdrawing from the world and denying to the body every pleasure, and harassing it so as not to do its will, suddenly we see egoism appearing as a disease of the soul, most often as *disobedience*, as *self-complacency*, as *grumbling*, and so on. In all these is hidden the ugliness of egoism. Examine each one of these and you will see its ugliness. Less often egoism manifests itself as a *demand*, as a *claim*, as a *right*, as a *desire*, as *vanity*, as *ambition*."

All these are forms of egoism. Let each one examine himself remarks St. Nectarios, and see if he has any of them. If he finds that he has, he should take care to uproot it, lest it grow into greater passions, rendering his spiritual striving fruitless.

In speaking of "passions (*páthe*), he distinguishes two kinds: "passions of the *soul*" and "passions of the *body*." In the writings of the Church Fathers, the following are often cited as "passions of the soul:" pride, vainglory, despondency, sorrow, anger, and greed. Cited as "passions of the body" are gluttony and fornication. The same names are given to the *vices* that grow out of them.

"Passions" are evil feelings, emotions or impulses that deviate from the purpose for which God gave them to man. When *feelings* are in accord with the Divine purpose they are said to be "according to nature" (*katá physin*). When they deviate from the Divine purpose, when they are deformed, they are said to be "contrary to nature" (*pará physin*). This is the traditional Orthodox view, which St. Nectarios follows. He says that God created all things very good (*kalá lian*—Genesis 1:31). He gave the feelings for a definite purpose or end. When the feelings function in accord with Divine Law, in accord with the reason for their existence, they constitute *moral power* and do not disturb the peace of the soul. They contribute to the work of the virtues. However, when the *feelings* function not for the purpose for which they were given by God, but contrary to it, contrary to nature, for our irrational gratification, they take on a sinful character and disturb the peace of the soul. Such feelings are properly called "passions."

St. Nectarios gives counsels for effectively dealing with passions. First of all, we must exercise careful *inner observation*. We must watch and see if any passions are present in our heart, in our soul. If there are, we must *wrestle* with them, *struggle* against them, against sin.

The Saint does not give examples. I shall give some that help one get a clear idea of the distinction between feelings that are "according to nature" and those that are "contrary to nature" and are called "passions." Anger is *according* to nature and hence good when we direct it against some bad habit of ours, in order to free ourselves from it. Anger is *contrary* to nature when we direct it against our fellow men. The same is true of hatred. Sorrow, also, may be either according to God or according to the world. "Sorrow according to God works to repentance," whereas "sorrow according to the world works death," as the Apostle Paul says (2 Corinthians 7:9-11). St. Nectarios says that sorrow, when excessive, is irrational (*álogos*) and comes from the Devil.

As to the outcome of our struggle with the passions, he says: "If in the struggle you are victorious, the uprising of the passions becomes an occasion of new joy and peace. On the other hand, if you are defeated—may this not happen—there results sorrow and agitation. However, if you return to the struggle and persist in it, peace within you will return." Further, he advises: "Do not despair. Gradually, with God's help the passions will be uprooted."

The combatant against the passions succeeds when, in addition to inner *attention* and *struggle,* he has recourse to *prayer*. He reminds his reader of the saying of our Savior:

"Be vigilant and pray, in order that ye enter not into temptation" (Matthew 26: 41).

Blessed Nectarios also gives counsels about "thoughts" (*logismoí*). Both passions and vices have as their starting point "thoughts." First comes into the mind some *bare thought* (*psilós logismós*) of an evil nature. When such a thought is allowed to *linger* in the mind it becomes a "passionate thought" (*empathés logismós*), by being warmed by a feeling of *assent* (*syngatáthesis*). This analysis appears in the *Ladder* of St. John Climacos and in the *Philokalia,* works that had been studied by our Saint.

Now when a passion is allowed to manifest itself again and again *overtly*, in acts, it becomes a *habit*, a fixed trait of character (*héxis*), and is called a *vice* (*kakía*). Vices are very difficult to uproot.

"Thoughts" have various origins: God, the senses, especially sight and hearing, demonic suggestion, etc. Regarding the latter, St. Nectarios counsels: "Do *not* let them *linger* in your mind, do not *assent* to them, but immediately *repel* them and *pray unceasingly.*"

This counsel is followed by an exhortation to *Confession.* In his letters to the nuns at Aegina his exhortation is brief but emphatic. In a book that he published long before he wrote the letters, and was available to the nuns, he devoted two chapters to a discussion of Confession. The title of the book is *Concerning Care of the Soul.*[1] In it he says at the outset: "Confession is necessary because: (a) it is a Commandment

---

[1] *Perí Epimeleías tes Psychés*, Athens, 1894.

of God; and (b) it restores peace between God and man; and (c) it benefits a person morally and spiritually."[1]

Regarding the third point, he remarks: "He who is confessed grows spiritually, first, because through the teaching of the Confessor the knowledge of the Confessor is gradually transmitted to the individual who is confessed; and second, because the mind of the latter, being cleansed of the darkness of sin and deception, is illuminated, receives the wonders of God, and develops."[2]

Seen in this light, remarks St. Nectarios, Confession "is the saving medicine of society, because it can save many souls from perdition, freeing them from delusion, from improper images and evil thoughts.... Hence, the Confessor is the moral physician of society. He alone has the power to prevent all the evils that today plague mankind."[3]

I might add here, parenthetically, that the efficacy of Confession in restoring and preserving the health of the mind has also been emphasized by the blessed Elder Gabriel Dionysiatis (1886-1983). Thus, he says: "We take tender care of the body and neglect the soul to the point of insensibility. If we fall slightly sick, or the idea enters into our mind that something is wrong in our body, we hastern to doctors, X-rays, and hot spring spas. We spare neither effort nor time, nor expense until we are informed that we are well. And all this for the mortal body. But for the immortal soul no positive care, no diagnosis, no visit to the spiritual clinic.... Confession gives purity to the soul, which is daily polluted by sin, whether by

[1] *Ibid.*, p. 78.
[2] *Ibid.*, p. 90.
[3] *Ibid.*, pp. 90-91.

deed, word, or thought. It is the bath of the soul that prepares man to receive the great Mysterion of Divine Communion. This is food for the soul, the Bread of Life."[1]

From I what have said about *vices, passions,* and *thoughts,* it is evident that according to St. Nectarios, those who desire to make progress in the spiritual life "must," according to his phrase, "struggle with themselves." They must struggle against their vices and passions, especially pride, and against their bad and useless thoughts. This struggle is part of what is called in Orthodox writings *askesis,* which consists of certain *bodily and mental practices.*

Bodily practices are valuable instruments for the acquisition of the virtues of the soul. St. Nectarios makes reference to *fasting, vigils, prostrations, reading religious works,* and *chanting.* He emphasizes that "bodily practices" are *means* for the attainment of the goal of the spiritual striver, not the goal itself. The goal is perfection, holiness, union with God, salvation.

He advises *avoidance of excesses* in the bodily practices of fasting, vigils, and prostrations. The needs of the body for its preservation in a state of good health must be taken into consideration. We must be careful not to cause harm to the body. He warns that beginners must not undertake great bodily askesis, one equal to that which is described in the lives of those who attained perfection or made great progress in the spiritual life. Great bodily askesis, he observes, presupposes great moral virtues that sustain the body intact. Beginners

---

[1] Quoted from my book *Blessed Elder Gabriel Dionysiatis* (Vol. 13 of my series *Modern Orthodox Saints*), Belmont, Massachusetts, 1999, p. 151.

must first strengthen their soul through the cultivation of the virtues of the soul and afterward proceed to greater bodily askesis. Otherwise there is danger of undermining the health of the body, or of falling spiritually through pride in one's extreme bodily askesis.[1]

As an example of how excesses are to be avoided the Saint gives to the Abbess the following advice with regard to food: "If someone of the young nuns is hungry in the evening, let her have a little bread and water, because she is still growing physically and must not be deprived of necessary nourishment, lest the body he harmed."

With regard to *vigils* he counsels the Abbess: "Church services are good, and I pray to God to give you strength. But perhaps the sisters are exhausted by them. If you notice that some of them are weakened by them, shorten the services somewhat."

He ascribes much value to *psalmody* or chanting, which is prayer involving the body. Through its sublime content, the beauty of the melodies and rhythms, psalmody uplifts our intellect and our emotions, giving us spiritual joy. Thus it invigorates both the soul and the body. In some of his letters he mentions that he composed some hymns to the Most Holy Theotokos and sent them to the nuns believing that they would fill their hearts with joy. To this joy he ascribed great value for both the soul and the body, as did St. Basil, St. John Chrysostom, St. John Climacos, and other Fathers of the Church.

[1] Cf. *Klimax*, Discourse 4, par. 119; English editon (*Ladder*), Step 4, par. 118.

Basil wrote: "The state of the soul in which there is joy and no sorrow is a boon that is bestowed by the consolation of hymns."[1] Chrysostom says: "Nothing uplifts the soul so much and gives it wings, and frees it from worldly cares, as much as divine song.... This gives the soul at once both pleasure and benefit."[2] Similarly, John Climacos remarks: "When there is psalmody despondency does not make its appearance."[3] And Neilos the Ascetic says: "Psalmody calms the passions and remedies the disorderly condition (*akrasía*) of the body."[4]

It is important that we have spiritual joy in our heart and that we transmit it to others. St. Nectarios emphasized this. Thus, in one of his letters to Abbess Xenia he wrote: "Realize that your cheerfulness gladdens the faces of the Sisters and renders the Convent a paradise. On the other hand, your depression and sullenness are transmitted to the other Sisters, and joyfulness is banished from that paradise. Learn, therefore, that the joy and cheerfulness of the Sisters depend upon you, and it is your duty to preserve these in their hearts. Do this even at times by forcing yourself. I counsel you not to surrender yourself to sorrowful fantasies, because this greatly depresses the hearts of the Sisters. Your reward will be great if you become to them a cause of cheerfulness. I give you this advice because I myself have it as a principle in my life. And

---

[1] *The Letters*, Loeb Classical Library, Vol. I, Letter 2, p. 13.

[2] Migne, *Patrologia Graeca*, Vol. 55, 156-157A.

[3] *Klimax*, Athens, 1979, Discourse 13, p. 81, par. 8. English editions of the *Ladder* have mistranslated this statement by inserting the word "no" before psalmody: "When there is no psalmody, then despondency does not make its appearance." This is the opposite of what the Greek text says!

[4] *Philokalia*, Athens, Vol. 1, 1957, p. 184.

I want my disciples also to have it as a principle. When you gladden the heart of your neighbor, much more of your Sister nun who has renounced everything, you may be sure that you please God much more than when you occupy yourself with extreme forms of askesis."

Now in order for a person to have joy within himself so as to be able to evoke it in others, he must be healthy in soul and body. For this and other reasons, besides giving advice for the care of the *soul* Nectarios gave counsels for keeping the *body* healthy or restoring it to health. In most of his letters to the Abbess and other nuns he shows great concern for their health and gives counsels for it.

Thus, in one of his letters he says: "Health is the first thing you must have. You need health in order to work spiritually.... Health is the self-propelled chariot that leads the spiritual athlete to the goal of the struggle. If you are healthy you will make progress. If you are not healthy your efforts are in vain."

For the preservation of one's health, our Saint emphasizes the need of *moderation*. "Flee from extremes," he counsels. "Extremes" are in the form of either *excess* or *deficiency*. Examples are, eating too much or too little, sleeping too much or too little, and exercising too much or not at all. It might be noted that St. Nectarios wrote a book entitled *Concerning True and Pseudo Education* in which there is a chapter on *Gymnastic*. He teaches the need of physical exercise done in moderation. Such exercise, he says, "increases the bodily powers for the sake of fulfilling the demands of the spirit and the performing of one's duties."[1]

[1] *Perí ton Apotelesmáton tes Alethoús kai Pseudoús Morphóseos*, Athens, 1894, pp. 18-19.

In his Letters he calls attention to the need of *good diet*. He particularly emphasizes the value of whole wheat bread, chickpeas, onions, and garlic—foods whose health promoting value is widely recognized today. For those who are weak he recommends eggs and milk. He advises the sick to follow the instructions of the physician, to have themselves crossed with sacred relics, and to have prayers recited invoking the help of God.

By following diligently the sagacious counsels of St. Nectarios, set forth in this lecture, a spiritual striver is bound to make great progress towards perfection.

CHAPTER FOUR

The Spiritual Strivers' Church in the Home[*]

The expression "the church in the home" is taken from the Epistle of the Apostle Paul to the Colossians where, in the fourth chapter, he says: "Give my greetings to the brethren at Laodicea and to Nympha and the church in her house." The word *ekklesía* ("church") in this verse refers to the faithful who come together in the home of Nympha in the form of a spiritual Christian gathering (*synaxis*). Throughout this talk I will be using both this meaning for the word "church," as well as for signifying a home transformed into a type of Christian temple to the degree this is possible.

There are families that have built a chapel inside their home—a type of small Christian church with an iconostasis, a Holy Table, and all that is required to conduct the Divine Liturgy. In general, these are families of great piety that are

---

[*] An address given to a Greek-speaking audience at the Church of Saint George in Lynn, Massachusetts, at the invitation of the priest of that parish, Father George Tsoucalas, on the Fifth Sunday of the Lent, March 13, 1997.

66

well off and have large homes. This is not the situation I have in mind when I use the phrase "church in the home." I am simply referring to certain things we should have in our homes which are found and used in an Orthodox church that aid in our coming to greater knowledge of our Orthodox faith and in our efforts to progress in the life in Christ. I will explain each of these one by one.

THE CROSS

I begin with a brief discussion on the use of the Cross. During my recent pilgrimage to the Holy Mountain of Athos, the very devout and wise abbot of the Holy Monastery of Gregoriou, Archimandrite George (Kapsanis) gave me several of the spiritually beneficial books he has written. In one of these he speaks at length about the Cross. Published by the Holy Mountain in 1993, its title is *The Cross of Christ and Its Meaning in Our Lives*. A small excerpt from this work contains valuable teachings on our subject and makes an excellent beginning for this lecture. Father George writes:

"The Holy Cross is the most holy Sign and Symbol of our Faith. All of our *Holy Mysteria* end with the invocation (*epíklesis*) of the Holy Spirit and the seal of the Cross—Baptism, Chrismation, the Holy Eucharist. All priestly blessings are made in the form of the cross. Our holy churches, the holy vessels and vestments are sanctified by the Holy Cross.... The Cross is the most faithful companion of every Orthodox Christian from the moment of birth until death. Even the grave of a Christian is blessed by the Cross. We make the sign of the Cross frequently, we bear the Cross on our breast, and have it in our homes, our automobiles, and in the places in which we work."

To these important observations, Archimandrite George adds several splendid verses from the *Exaposteilárion* hymn chanted at the feast of the Elevation of the Holy and Life-Giving Cross:

"The Cross, guardian of the whole earth;
The Cross, beauty of the Church;
The Cross, strength of kings;
The Cross, support of the faithful;
The Cross, glory of angels
and wounder of demons."

In the minds of Orthodox Christians, the Cross, which symbolizes the Crucifixion of our Savior Jesus Christ, is also closely connected with His Resurrection and serves to remind us of this joyous event. For this reason, we chant the following hymn on the feast day of the Cross:

We venerate thy Cross, O Master,
and glorify Thy most holy Resurrection.

It is worthy of note that in the central church (the *Katholikón*) of an Athonite monastery, the icon of the Resurrection is placed next to that of the Crucifixion above the Beautiful Gate—the main entrance into the Holy Bema through the iconostasis.

In accordance with everything we have said thus far concerning the Cross, it is a most excellent practice for Orthodox Christians of all ages to wear a small cross on our chests, either outside or beneath our clothing. Both when we are at home and away, we should always wear a cross, as something holy, as our protector, and as a perpetual reminder of our Savior Jesus Christ.

It would be ideal if our little crosses had etched upon them lightly the Crucifixion on one side and the Panagia holding the Infant Christ on the other. Until a few years ago, such finely carved wooden crosses were made by hand on the Holy Mountain by many of the hermit monks. Today, only a few monks work this craft anymore, since faster and cheaper (but of lower quality) methods of production exist. If we should ever go as pilgrims to the Holy Mountain, or if someone we know is going, it would be good for us to take the opportunity to acquire a cross of the older, handcrafted type. It would be best for us to avoid crucifixes of a Western type, in which Christ and the Panagia are depicted in high relief, like small statues. In a true Orthodox cross, the carving is of low relief, having the character of an icon in two dimensions.

In addition to the small cross we wear, we would do well also to have a larger cross with Christ depicted in the traditional Orthodox manner. On such a cross, the words "The King of Glory" are written across the top, and not "INBI," which stands for "Jesus the Nazarene, King of the Jews." The most appropriate place for this cross is on the iconostasis of our home.

Closely related to the Cross is the sign of the Cross we make by moving our right hand. We make the sign of the Cross during our morning and evening prayers, before we sit to eat, and again just after eating. Also, we always cross ourselves before reverently kissing the Cross or a holy icon.

We should cross ourselves with piety, with contrition, and in the true form of the Cross. We should never make the sign of the Cross hurriedly or mechanically as if we were strumming a guitar or mandolin.

Saint Cosmas Aitolos tells us how we are to make the sign of the Cross and gives us a beautiful explanation of the significance of this act in one of his "Teachings" (*Didachaí*), as his sermons are known. This great Missionary tells us: "My brothers, listen to how one's Cross is to be made and what it means. First, as the Holy Trinity is glorified in heaven by the Angels, so too should you bring your three fingers together. And being unable to ascend into heaven in order to venerate there, bring your hand to your forehead, which signifies heaven, and say in your heart: "As the Angels glorify the Holy Trinity in heaven, so too do I as a servant glorify and venerate the Holy Trinity."

«"And as your three fingers are each separate yet become as one, the Holy Trinity in the same way is three persons but one God. Lowering your hand to your abdomen, say: "I bow down before Thee and I venerate and worship Thee my Lord, for Thou didst condescend to become incarnate in the womb of the Theotokos for our sins. And raising your hand to your right shoulder you say: "I beseech Thee, my God, to forgive me and put me on Thy right with the righteous." And placing your hand on your left shoulder say: "I implore Thee my Lord, do not put me on left with the sinners."»

THE ICONOSTASIS

Without exception, our homes should have an iconostasis in one of its rooms. It should contain a few icons, a Cross, a censer, a small candlestick, a small bottle with *hagiasmós,*

PHOTIOS KONTOGLOU
At his home study.

and a votive lamp. The iconostasis could be in the dining room, the living room, or some other room. My blessed teacher and friend Photios Kontoglou had his iconostasis in the dining room. Since his home was small, he used this room as an office and as a studio for painting icons. In one corner of the dining room, just across from the door, was a bookcase, full of books, whose top, along with the wall above made up the iconostasis. On top of the bookcase was a perpetually lit votive lamp (*akoímeto kandeli*, "unsleeping" lamp), several old icons, a large Book of the Gospels, an antique carved Cross, a small case with holy relics, and a silver case in the form of a life-sized human hand in which were relics of Saint Paraskevi. Among the icons were one of the Panagia holding the Child Christ and a miraculous icon of Saint Paraskevi. Several other icons were hung on the wall above.

It is a good practice to have icons in other rooms of the house as well. The humble home of devout Photios Kontoglou provided an excellent example: it had icons in the living room and in the bedroom, too. Holy icons should replace paintings and photographs that have a worldly and carnal expression.

Religious icons are of two types: the traditional or Byzantine style, and the innovative or "modern" style. The "modern" style has been influenced by the Papal Church and has a worldly character, not a spiritual one. In contrast, traditional icons have a spiritual nature; they express spiritual beauty, the beauty of the soul and the virtues. The "modern" style icons seek to express external, fleshly, and corruptible beauty. Traditional Byzantine icons are spiritually elevating; they lift the soul above the realm of the senses to the holy, the divine.

The "modern" icons of Western origin lack this spiritual character. Their theme is religious, but their expression is secular.

By all means, we should have small icons in our cars, which have become extensions of our homes. We most certainly need the protection of Christ and the Panagia.

THE KANDELI (VIGIL/VOTIVE LAMP)

The votive lamp used in our iconostasis should be of a traditional type that uses oil and not an electric bulb. It should be kept lit day and night. Such a lamp is an offering of honor to Christ, the Theotokos, and the Saints depicted in our icons. The maintenance of this lamp—replenishing its oil, regularly trimming the wick—becomes a kind of prayer. Being attentive to our votive lamp brings to mind God and the Saints, and thus becomes a part of the unceasing prayer commended to us by the Apostle Paul: "Pray without ceasing" (I Thessalonians 5:17).

INCENSE

As I mentioned earlier, we should also keep a small censer, made of ceramic or brass, among the things in our iconostasis. With this censer we should cense our icons in all the rooms of our home, especially on great feastdays, Saturday evenings, and Sundays. Orthodox Christians who are especially pious cense their homes every day in the morning and in the evening at the setting of the sun.

The beautiful fragrance of incense, especially the Athonite *moschothymíama*, evokes contrition and intensifies the prayers we say while censing, whether we say them out loud or in our hearts. Our prayer during this time becomes like the spiritual incense spoken of by the Prophet-King David who wrote: "Let my prayer arise as incense before Thee" (Psalm 140:2-Septuagint).

OUR LIBRARY OF RELIGIOUS BOOKS

Next to our iconostasis, or in some other place in our home, we should have a bookcase with religious books, even if it is only a small one. In the home of blessed Kontoglou there were two bookcases, one in the dining room under the iconostasis and another in the living room by the door that connected the two rooms. There he had an *analógion* or wooden stand such as the chanters use in church. On the upper part were a few liturgical books of the Church, such as the *Parakletike* and one of the *Menaia*,[1] while below he kept the other liturgical books used by the chanters. He used these books each morning and evening when he was unable to go to church and would chant the hymns appropriate for that day, for Photios was proficient in the sacred art of Byzantine chant. On evenings when I visited him and his very pious spouse Maria, if some bishop, priest, or priestmonk happened to be visiting, these books and the *analogion* were used by them and Photios to chant the Vespers.

The most useful books for our home library are:

[1] The *Parakletike* contains the weekly cycle of services in each of the eight modes of Byzantine chant. There are eight complete cycles, with hymns for each day, beginning on Saturday evening until the next Saturday, when the mode changes. The *Menaia* are twelve books corresponding to the twelve months of the year and contain the special hymns and troparia for each day's feast or commemorated saint.

a) *The Bible*, that is, the Old and New Testaments, in the original Septuagint Greek, and translated into purist modern Greek. For those who do not know Greek the old King James Version is recommended as the best.

b) *Synékdemos* or *Megále Hierá Synopsis*. This book is a treasure for the entire year. It contains prayers that are said in the morning, when we arise, and in the evening, before going to sleep, as well as prayers for before and after meals, the services of Sundays, that is, the Orthros, the Divine Liturgy, and the Vespers. In addition, it contains the Gospel and Epistle readings of the Sundays of the year and the services of the movable feasts during the periods of Great Lent, Holy Week, Pentecost, and much more.[1]

c) *The Great Horologion*. In this book may be found listed all the feast days of the year and the saints commemorated on each day. It contains the *Apolytikion* and *Kontakion* in honor of the saints of the Church for every day of the year. In addition, it contains Canons of Entreaty to the Panagia (e.g., the Akathistos Hymn), the Service of Preparation for Holy Communion, and a great deal more. The practice of opening the *Horologion* during our morning prayers and chanting the *Apolytikion* and *Kontakion* of that day's feast or honored saint is indeed God-pleasing. If we cannot chant, then we should read these hymns.

---

[1] This book is a compilation of excerpts from many of the Church's service books—the *Horologion*, the *Parakletike*, the *Menaia*. In its entirety it is not available in English, but selections may be found in different prayerbooks published by Holy Cross Orthodox Press, Holy Transfiguration Monastery of Boston, Holy Trinity Monastery in Jordanville, N.Y., and so on.

d) *Lives of the Saints.* St Ephraim the Syrian writes: "Blessed is he who cultivates good 'plants' in his soul, that is, the virtues and lives of the saints." St. John of the Ladder (Climacos) writes: "It is good for us to marvel at the struggles of the saints; by imitating them we will win salvation for ourselves." Reading such works grants rest and comfort to both soul and body. It elevates our thoughts and emotions and prepares us for contrite and fruitful prayer.

It is good to add other books to those I have mentioned: works written by the holy Fathers of the Church and theologians who teach correctly, works which explain the Dogmas, Canons, and Divine Mysteria of the Church, as well as its history. Similarly, it is good to have books in our library which teach us to discern soul-corrupting heresies, and which show us how to free ourselves from passions and vices and acquire the virtues.

The benefit we realize from our religious library will be in direct proportion to the use we make of it. The more we use it, the greater benefit we will receive. However, even the sight of these books can in some way be of benefit to us. St. Epiphanios, Bishop of Cyprus (4th century) says with respect to this: "The mere sight of these books renders us less inclined to sin and incites us to believe more firmly in righteousness" (from the *Gerontikón*, a book comprised of sayings of the Desert Fathers").

COLLECTION OF RECORDINGS OF ORTHODOX HYMNS
AND BYZANTINE MUSIC

Another very valuable aid in helping us to become better Christians is to possess and listen to tapes of traditional Orthodox chant, called Byzantine music. Through listening frequently to such music, we obtain great benefit for our souls, and also for our bodies. Concerning the spiritual benefit, Saint Basil the Great writes: "The consolations of hymns impart to the soul a state of gladness and tranquillity." Saint John Chrysostom writes: "Nothing uplifts the soul so much and gives it wings, and frees it from worldly cares, so much as divine song.... This gives at once both pleasure and benefit." Other holy Fathers have emphasized that psalmody (chanting) expels anger, despair, and sorrow, while exerting a calming influence on the other passions, as well as improving the condition of the body.

For a Christian to listen to tapes of Church hymns chanted in Byzantine style, by chanters with good voices, is truly a banquet that nourishes the soul, strengthening and elevating it, and is conducive to our twofold health. Audiotapes of this type may be found in the religious bookstores in Athens and Thessalonika, especially in those of the brotherhoods of theologians "*O Soter*" and "*Zoe*," while in America they may be obtained from Holy Cross Orthodox Bookstore in Brookline, Massachusetts.

Some of the excellent cantors who have made recordings are Theodoros Vasilikos, Lykourgos Angelopoulos, Georgios Syrkas, and Photis Kezentzis, who is presently Professor of Byzantine Music at Holy Cross Greek Orthodox School of Theology. Besides having good voices, they possess the Byzantine style of chanting. They chant reverently, with modesty and contrition, without pomp or ostentation. Their chanting constitutes prayer, by means of both the soul and the body.

By listening to such chanting regularly, and by chanting along with the tape, whoever has a good ear and voice may gradually learn to chant properly and beautifully in the traditional Orthodox manner. Especially valuable for learning Byzantine music are sets of eight cassettes with all the eight modes of Byzantine chant. The *protopsaltes* Photis Kezentzis and Theodoros Vasilikos have produced excellent recordings of this cycle. Each cassette has the Resurrectional (*Anastásima*) hymns of the Vespers and Orthros of the *Parakletike*.

A beautiful, spiritually beneficial practice is to chant on the days of the feasts, especially the great ones (such as Christmas, Theophany, the Annunciation, Palm Sunday, and Pascha) the related Apolytikia at the time of the prayer before dinner and supper. We know most of these by memory, and we may look in the *Synekdemos* or the *Horologion* to find them: "Thy Nativity, O Christ our God," chanted on Christmas; "When Thou, O Lord, wast baptized in the Jordan," of Theophany (Epiphany); "Today is the crown of our salvation," of the feast of the Annunciation; and the troparion "Giving us before Thy Passion an assurance of the general resurrection, Thou hast raised Lazarus from the dead, O Christ our God," of the Saturday of the holy and righteous Lazarus, as well as on Palm Sunday. And all of us know the troparion of Pascha quite well: "Christ is risen from the dead, by death hath He trampled down death, and on those in the graves hath He bestowed life."

COLLECTION OF RECORDED SERMONS
THAT ARE SPIRITUALLY BENEFICIAL

In addition to our collection of cassettes of Byzantine music, it would be good for us to have a collection of cassettes with spiritually beneficial sermons. We should listen to sermons by recognized *hierokerykes* (those with a blessing to sermonize), such as Augustinos Kantiotis, Bishop of Phlorina, Greece, and Archimandrite Haralampos Vasilopoulos, founder of the "Panhellenic Orthodox Union" and of the newspaper *Orthodoxos Typos*. When we listen to such talks with care and attention, we learn many things about our Orthodox faith and the way in which we should live it so that it will become alive, manifesting itself through deeds. By listening to them we also learn about spiritually harmful heresies such as those of Papism, Protestantism, Jehovah's Witnesses, and the reasons we should avoid them.

Heresy means false teaching, which is to the soul what poison is to the body. It separates the soul from God and leads it to perdition.

For this reason, we should be very careful about the cassettes we obtain or accept from others. We should seek the counsel of our spiritual father and guide, or of a reputable theologian. We should only possess and listen to tapes by Orthodox theologians whose spirituality shines forth, who are of impeccable moral character, and whose knowledge of the Orthodox faith is firm.

Videotapes, Televisions, and Radios

Besides the above-mentioned audiocassettes, there are also videocassettes or videotapes. Only a few videotapes are appropriate for an Orthodox home, those which present Orthodox shrines, e.g., Byzantine churches, their icons (panels and murals), monasteries such as those on the Holy Mountain, Meteora, the Holy Land (Palestine and Sinai), as well as lectures by spiritual persons, whom we see speaking in churches, church halls or shrines. It would be prudent to avoid Roman Catholic videos such as "The Passion of Christ," for example, in which the portrayals are by actors. For us Orthodox, only a pious priest with traditional vestments and beard portrays the image of Christ, not actors. It is unnecessary for me to stress that in an Orthodox home there should never be videos portraying immodest scenes and unseemly dialogue and music.

What I said about videos is equally applicable to television. When compared with television, videotapes are advantageous in that we can choose them ourselves in the stores where they are sold, as opposed to television, which presents us with whatever is being shown at the moment we turn it on—good or bad. Inappropriate sights and sounds predominate. Usually, whatever one sees and hears on television has the effect of polluting our vision, our hearing, and soul: crimes, robberies, murders, obscene and sinful acts of all kinds, impassioned and brazen words spoken in anger, endless and tiring commercials, and other things of this type.

Also, frequent and prolonged television watching causes damage to our eyes and health in general. The radiation emitted from the screen is harmful to us. Blessed is the home that does not have a television, or if it does have one makes extremely limited use of it, perhaps once a day to learn about the weather, the world news, or to watch an educational program.

The radio, which in our time is found in virtually all homes, is not as damaging as the television, because it is directed only to the sense of hearing, whereas television appeals *also* to the sense of sight, "the king of the five senses." The radio does not emit harmful radiation, as does a television, especially a color television. However, this invention of modern technology must also be used sparingly and with great discretion. There are many who wish to listen to the radio day and night, and indeed quite loud, without discerning between good and bad broadcasts. This is one of the worst habits we can have and is catastrophic for the soul. The Apostle Paul writes: "Pray without ceasing," which means to pray without interruption. How is it possible to pray continually and think about God, His Saints, their spiritually beneficial teachings and examples, while listening to the vain and spiritually corrupting words broadcast on the radio? Impossible! What do we usually hear on the radio? Shouting, noise, tumults, vain talk, useless banter, and sexually provocative songs by men and women of lesser morals.

It would be wise to limit use of the radio to the holy sermons of Orthodox speakers, Byzantine music, patriotic programs, and programs with community and worldwide news. In this way we can achieve relative quiet in our homes, which is indispensable for concentration and prayer. In this way, our home will more closely resemble a church, which is characterized by St. John Chrysostom as a safe harbor for the soul. He writes:

"The church is a spiritual harbor for the soul. If someone were to examine his conscience within the Church, he would find great peace. He is neither troubled by anger, nor plagued by despair, nor defiled by the passion of vainglory. These wild beasts are a all quieted as if by some divine charm."[1]

[1] Migne, *Patrologia Graeca*, Vol. 49, col. 363.

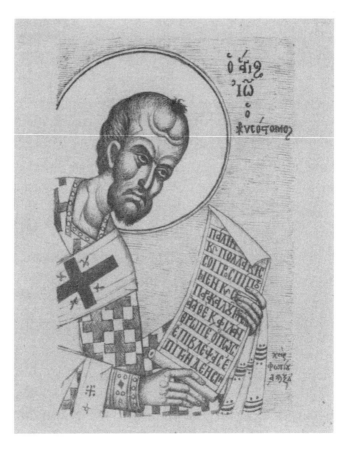

Sᴛ. Jᴏʜɴ Cʜʀʏsᴏsᴛᴏᴍ
Icon by Photios Kontoglou. 1961.

PRAYER

Quiet and stillness in our homes makes it possible for us to pray more and with greater fruitfulness.

I have already touched on the topic of prayer at various points in this talk. At this juncture I would like to speak about a type of prayer that is easy for each of us to say frequently. It is a very short prayer and requires neither great memory to remember its words, nor any special circumstances in order to say it. We can say it anywhere and at every hour of the day. This prayer is called "mental prayer" (*noerá proseuché*), or the "Jesus prayer" (*Euché Iesoú*).

It is called "mental" because we say it with our mind and not out loud with our mouth. It is called the "Jesus prayer" because we call upon our Lord Jesus Christ, saying silently: "Lord Jesus Christ, Son of God, have mercy upon me."

When we grow accustomed to this prayer, and feel its sweetness and benefits, there will arrive in us the strong desire to say it frequently. An excellent practice is to take our prayer rope (one with a hundred knots) each evening, before lying down to sleep and to sit on the edge of the bed, or in a chair, and say this prayer for ten or more minutes. The prayer rope is held in the left hand and each time we say "Lord Jesus Christ, Son of God, have mercy upon me," we move one knot along the rope with our thumb. In this way, we keep track of how many times we say the prayer. Each time we complete a cycle on the prayer rope, we make the sign of the Cross with our right hand.

In the *Philokalia* compiled and edited by St. Macarios of Corinth and St. Nicodemos the Hagiorite, is found a remarkable chapter entitled "Explanation of the *Kyrie Eléison* (Lord have mercy)."[1] The author of this short work tells us *what* we ask of Christ when we call upon Him to have mercy upon us. Among other things he says the following: "The mercy of God is nothing else, but the *grace* of the All-Holy Spirit, which we sinners have need to ask of God and to cry out without ceasing, 'Lord have mercy,' which means, 'Have compassion on me, Lord, on me the sinner in the pitiful condition in which I find myself; take me back into Thy grace. Grant me a spirit of strength so that I may be strengthened and withstand the temptations of the devil and the evil habit of sin. Grant me a spirit of self-correction that I might correct myself, that I might come into knowledge of myself and rectify myself. Grant me a spirit of fear that I might keep Thy commandments. Grant me a spirit of love that I might love Thee and no longer separate myself from Thee. Grant me a spirit of peace to keep my soul peaceful and quiet. Grant me a spirit of purity that it might keep me pure from every defilement. Grant me a spirit of meekness that I might be gentle among my brother Christians and kept from anger. Grant me a spirit of humility, that I might not be proud.'"

Many saints of the Church recommend this mental prayer to us. They emphasize that everyone can practice the mental prayer, "Lord Jesus Christ, Son of God, have mercy upon me," anywhere and at all times. They also note that this prayer brings us great consolation, inner peace, and support from God.

In the monasteries and hermitages of the Holy Mountain of Athos the monks practice this mental prayer in the evening

[1] Vol. 5, Athens, 1963, p. 69.

and after midnight while shut in their cells with only the small light from their votive lamps. Those of us who live in the world, and lack the ability to keep such a vigil daily, can begin by praying mentally for five minutes each evening, slowly increasing the time to ten or more minutes. The degree to which one might occupy himself with this prayer each night will depend on the conditions in his life and on his zeal. Without godly zeal, there can be no progress in our spiritual life, in our journey toward virtue and salvation.

The practices that I have mentioned will all serve to increase our zeal. There are a few more I would like to mention briefly, such as regular church attendance and careful selection of the people with whom we choose to associate in our homes, whether they be relatives or non-family members.

Regular church attendance, our presence in the church at Orthros, Divine Liturgy, Vespers, and at other services such as Paraklesis, Evcheleon, Confession, and Holy Communion contribute greatly to our acquisition of a robust spiritual *phrónema* (mindset). However, it is necessary for us to participate in these services with attention, piety, and contrition.

As for the persons whom we invite into our homes, we must take care that they are spiritual people, good Orthodox, and not heretics. We are advised thus by the Apostle Paul who says: "Do not be deceived: 'Bad company ruins good morals'" (I Corinthians 15:33). In other words, bad companions spoil one's character. And as we read in the Old Testament: "With the holy man thou wilt be holy, and with the perfect man, thou wilt be perfect, and with the excellent, thou wilt be excellent, and with the perverted man, thou wilt be perverted" (2 Kings 22,26-27; Septuagint). Similar statements have been made by ancient Greek philosophers such as Socrates, Plato, and Aristotle.

I will close my talk by drawing attention to the three great enemies that will not allow us to be successful in the spiritual life. These enemies are (1) ignorance, (2) forgetfulness, and (3) sloth, or lack of zeal. St. Mark the Ascetic, one of the holy Fathers of the *Philokalia*, calls these three great enemies, the "three powerful giants of the Devil" that lead us to perdition. The things I have described in this talk all work together to combat and repulse them. They combat our ignorance concerning the Orthodox faith and replace it with knowledge of the faith and the Truth that leads to salvation. They combat forgetfulness by reminding us constantly of our faith—through holy icons, through chanting, through spiritually beneficial readings and sermons. All of these bring to the mind, in the words of the Apostle Paul, "whatsoever things are honest, whatsoever things are just, whatsoever things are pure, whatsoever things are lovely, whatsoever things are of good report: if there be any virtue, and if there be any praise" (Philippians 4:8).

Combating and expelling ignorance, forgetfulness, and sloth in this way, we become "fervent in spirit" (Romans, 12:11), full of godly zeal, and can progress in the spiritual life.

Index of Proper Names

Index of Subjects

purity, 34, 35, 44, 47-48, 51, 60, 84

quiet, 83, 84

radio, 46, 79-81
reading, 41-42, 43, 49, 61 , 86
reason, 50
renunciation, 37
repentance, 58
resolve, 35, 37
Rudder, the, 25

sacred poetry, 26
sacred relics, 65, 72
saints, 22ff., 35-36
salvation, 14, 15, 61, 76, 85, 86
sanctification, 15ff.
self-complacency, 56
self-control, 19-20, 50
self-correction, 84
self-discipline, 38
self-examination, 55-56
self-restraint, 38, 40, 44
senses, 46-47, 59, 72, 79-81
sermons, 78-80, 81, 86
sin, 32, 50, 57, 58, 60, 70, 76, 84
sloth, 50, 86
smoking, 47
sorrow, 44, 57, 58, 63, 77
soul, 13-14, 18, 42, 43, 44, 45, 47, 50, 55, 57, 60-63, 79, 80, 81
spiritual father, guide, 79